Mathematics

Book 3

- *Odd numbers*
- *Even numbers*
- *Place value*
- *Time*
- *Ordinal numbers*
- *Cardinal numbers*
- *Roman numbers*
- *Addition*
- *Subtraction*
- *Multiplication*
- *Division*

Purnima Sharma, M.A., B.Ed.

Fun with Numbers

1. Fill in the numbers that come in between.

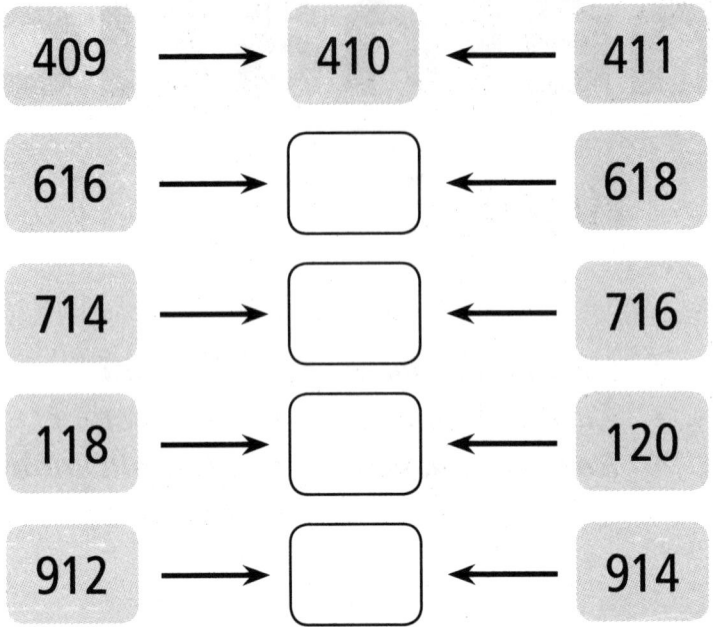

2. Complete the given series of numbers by skip counting.

20	☆	40	☆	60	☆	80	☆	100
120	☆	140	☆	160	☆	180	☆	200
210	220	☆	☆	250	260	☆	☆	290
300	☆	310	☆	☆	☆	350	360	☆
380	☆	400	410	420	☆	☆	450	460
470	☆	490	500					

3. What comes before and what comes after?

6 → 7	100 → ☐
18 → ☐	229 → ☐
40 → ☐	330 → ☐
84 → ☐	499 → ☐
79 → ☐	999 → ☐

4. What comes before these numbers?

Example:- 14 ← 15

☐ ← 270	☐ ← 413
☐ ← 720	☐ ← 660
☐ ← 950	☐ ← 160
☐ ← 218	

5. Write the missing numbers. Skip 10 numbers to fill the stars in part A and skip 50 numbers backwards to fill the blanks in part B.

A ↓

INCREASING ORDER

401	411	421	431	441
402	☆	422	☆	442
403	413	423	433	443
☆404	414	☆	434	☆
405	415	425	435	445
406	☆	426	☆	446
407	417	427	437	447
☆	418	☆	438	☆
409	419	429	439	449
410	☆	430	☆	450

B ↓

DECREASING ORDER

500	450	☆	350
495	445	395	345
490	☆	390	☆
485	435	385	335
480	430	☆	330
475	425	375	☆
470	☆	370	320
465	415	365	☆
460	410	☆	310
455	405	355	☆

Odd and Even Numbers

Even numbers are those which can be divided by 2 like 4, 6, 8,10. Odd numbers are those which are not divisible by 2 like 3, 5, 7, 9.

Remember

1. Even + Even = Even   2 + 2   = 4
2. Even - Even = Even   4 - 2   = 2
3. Even × Even = Even   6 x 2   = 12
4. Even + Odd = Odd

   12 + 5   = $\boxed{17}$

5. Even - Odd = Odd

   6 - 3   = $\boxed{3}$

6. Even × Odd = Even

   4 × 3   = $\boxed{12}$

Similarly:-

1. Odd + Odd = Even   1 + 3 = 4
2. Odd - Odd = Even   7 − 5 = 2
3. Odd × Odd = Odd   3 × 5 = 15

Remember

<u>Zero</u> is considered to be an <u>even</u> number.

1. Here are a few numbers. Make a star on the odd numbers and underline the even numbers.

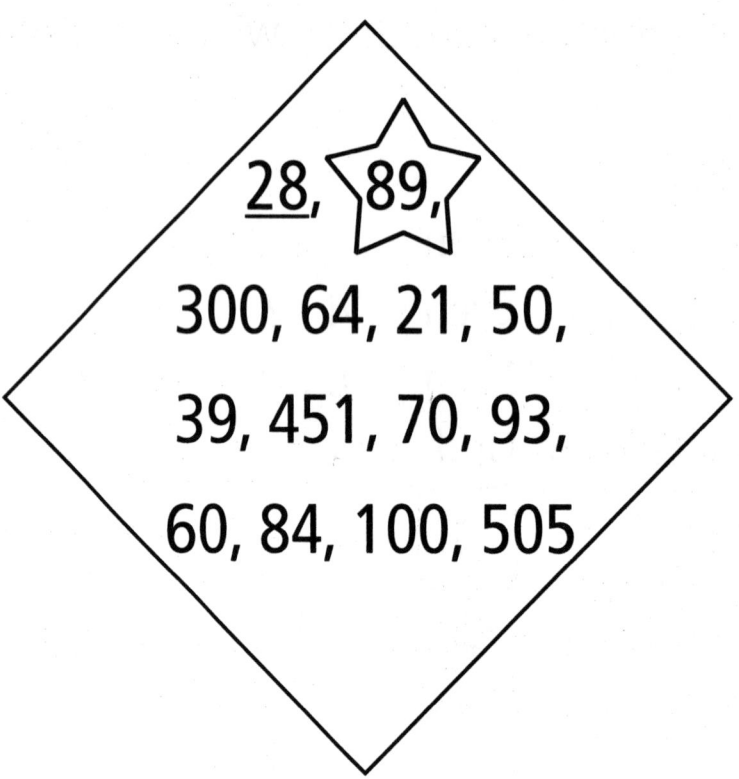

28, 89, 300, 64, 21, 50, 39, 451, 70, 93, 60, 84, 100, 505

2. Tick the even numbers.

17	24	30	29	67
9	14	13	13	61
21	32	16	16	50
60	54	15	100	11

3. Tick the even numbers and cross the odd numbers.

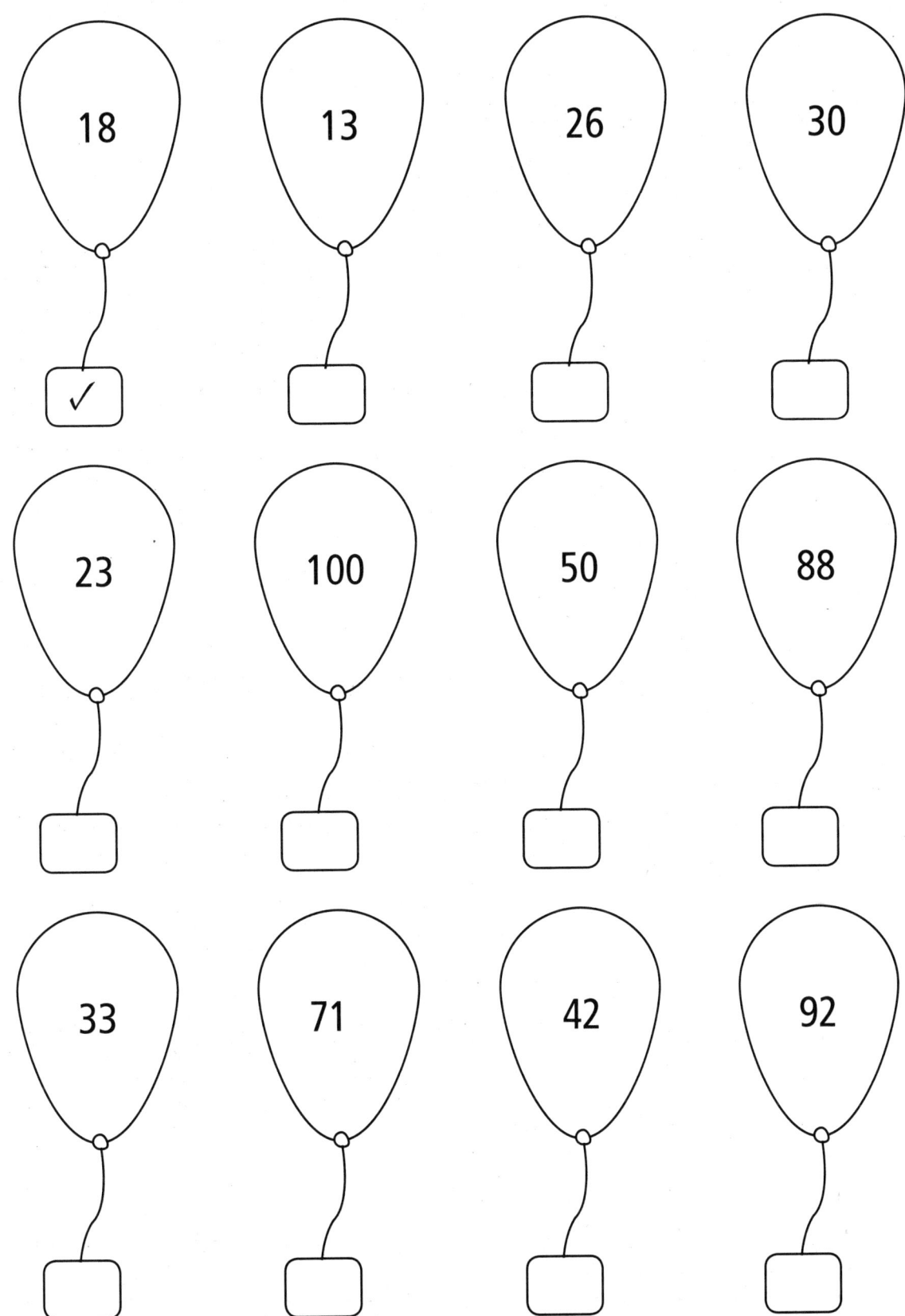

Place Value

The value of where a digit is in a number is called its **Place value**.

Example:-

Place value of 9999 (Largest 4 digit number)

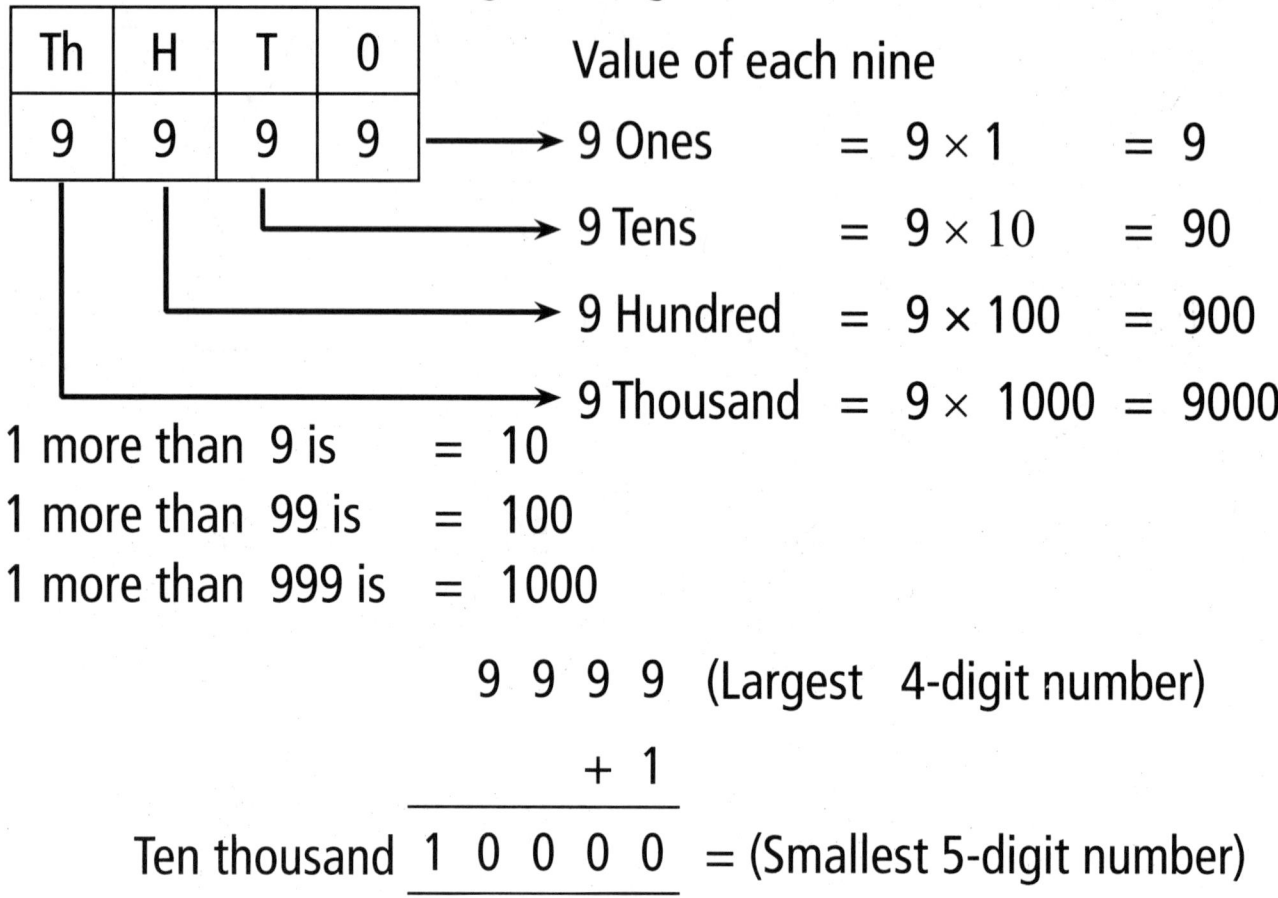

1 more than 9 is = 10
1 more than 99 is = 100
1 more than 999 is = 1000

$$9\ 9\ 9\ 9 \quad \text{(Largest 4-digit number)}$$
$$+\ 1$$
$$\text{Ten thousand } 1\ 0\ 0\ 0\ 0 = \text{(Smallest 5-digit number)}$$

$$9\ 9\ 9\ 9\ 9 \quad \text{(Greatest 5-digit number)}$$
$$+\ 1$$
$$\text{One lakh } 1\ 0\ 0\ 0\ 0\ 0 = \text{(Smallest 6-digit number)}$$

Lakh	Thousand		One		
L	T Th	Th	H	T	O
LAKH	TEN THOUSAND	THOUSAND	HUNDRED	TENS	ONES
Smallest 6-digit 1	0	0	0	0	0
Greatest 6-digit 9	9	9	9	9	9

1. Write the numbers in their correct places and their number names too. One is done for your help.

a. 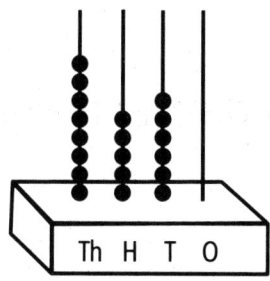 ← 8560

Number name _____

b. 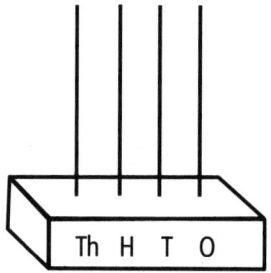 ← 7859

Number name _____

c. 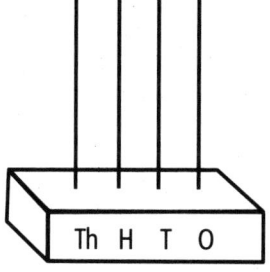 ← 9876

Number name _____

d. 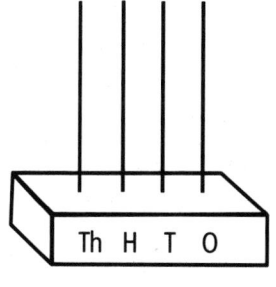 ← 6652

Number name _____

2. Write each number in its correct place. One has been done for you.

Example:-

a. 57,389 = (fifty seven thousand three hundred and eighty nine)

    5   Ten thousand
    7   Thousand
    3   Hundred
    8   Tens
    9   Ones

b. 99,989

    _____ Ten thousand
    _____ Thousand
    _____ Hundred
    _____ Tens
    _____ Ones

c. 84,567

    _____ Ten thousand
    _____ Thousand
    _____ Hundred
    _____ Tens
    _____ Ones

Write in Words

Write the number names of the given numbers.

	Numbers		Number names
1.	0	=	zero
2.	312	=	_____
3.	420	=	_____
4.	779	=	_____
5.	240	=	_____
6.	498	=	_____
7.	6914	=	_____
8.	8706	=	_____
9.	1080	=	_____
10.	9999	=	_____
11.	840	=	_____

Which is the largest 4-digit number?

= [   ]

Abacus

Depict the 4-digit numerals on the abacus and write their number names too. One has been done for you.

Example:- Numeral 5746

Step 1.   The digit in one's place is 6. So, we will draw 6 beads on the spike in one's place.

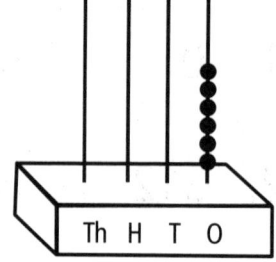

Step 2.   The digit in ten's place is 4. So, we will draw 4 beads on the spike in ten's place.

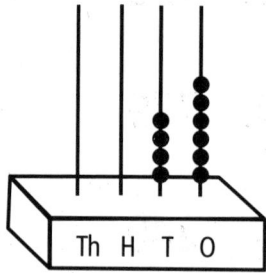

Step 3.   The digit in hundred's place is 7. So, we will draw 7 beads on the spike in hundred's place.

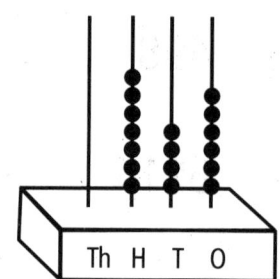

Step 4.   The digit 5 is in the thousand's place. So, we will draw 5 beads on the spike in thousand's place.

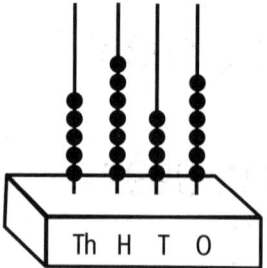

So the number name for 5746 is five thousand seven hundred and forty six.

1. 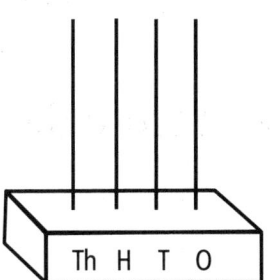 ← 6025

   Number name _____
   _____

2. 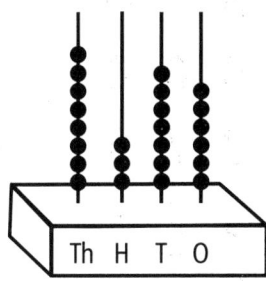 = Number [ ]
   = _____

3. 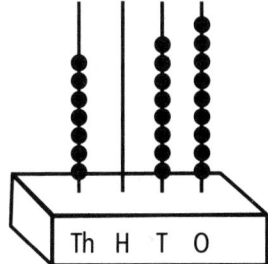 = Number [ ]
   = _____

4. 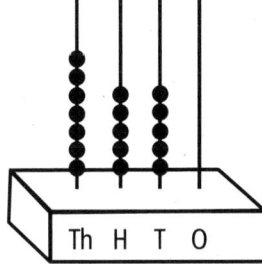 = Number [ ]
   = _____

5. 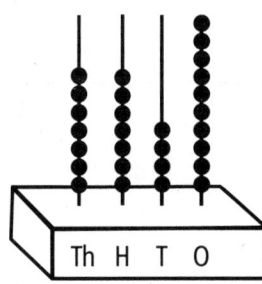 = Number [ ]
   = _____

Addition

Put the numbers in their right places. Add them and write the answer in words. One has been done for you.

Add:- 1000, 876 and 985

Note - Always write numbers from the right hand side
Th ← h ← ten ← one

```
   Th  H  T  O
    1  0  0  0
       8  7  6
+      9  8  5
   ─────────────
    2  8  6  1
   ─────────────
```

Answer: 2861
(Two thousand eight hundred and sixty one)

1. Add:- 6854, 975 and 459

```
   Th   H   T   O
    .   .   .   .
    .   .   .   .
+       .   .   .
   ──────────────
   ──────────────
```

Answer: _____
(_____)

2. Add:- 9854, 7650, 8923 and 854

	Th	H	T	O
	.	.	.	.
	.	.	.	.
	.	.	.	.
+		.	.	.

Answer: _____

(_____)

3. Add:- 10,000, 8976, 985 and 90

	Th	H	T	O
	.	.	.	.
	.	.	.	.
	.	.	.	.
+			.	.

Answer: _____

(_____)

4. Add:- 87630, 5432, 202 and 36

	Th	H	T	O
	.	.	.	.
	.	.	.	.
	.	.	.	.
+			.	.

Answer: _____

(_____)

Subtraction with Borrowing

Example:-

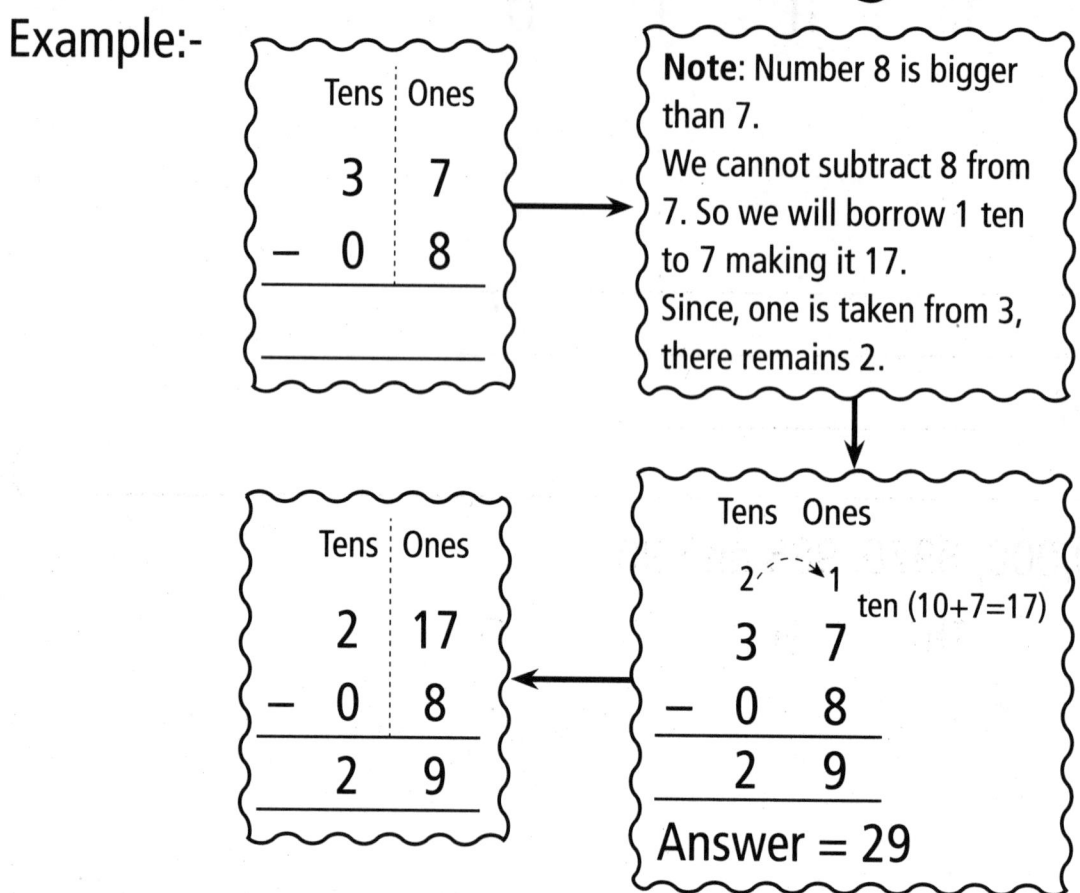

Note: Number 8 is bigger than 7.
We cannot subtract 8 from 7. So we will borrow 1 ten to 7 making it 17.
Since, one is taken from 3, there remains 2.

Answer = 29

Subtract:-

20 birds were eating grains. One of the them flew away. How many birds remained there?

Answer: ☐ birds remained

Subtraction Again

Arrange in columns and substract.

Remember

Check the number of digits and write the digits at their correct place from the right hand side.

Example:-

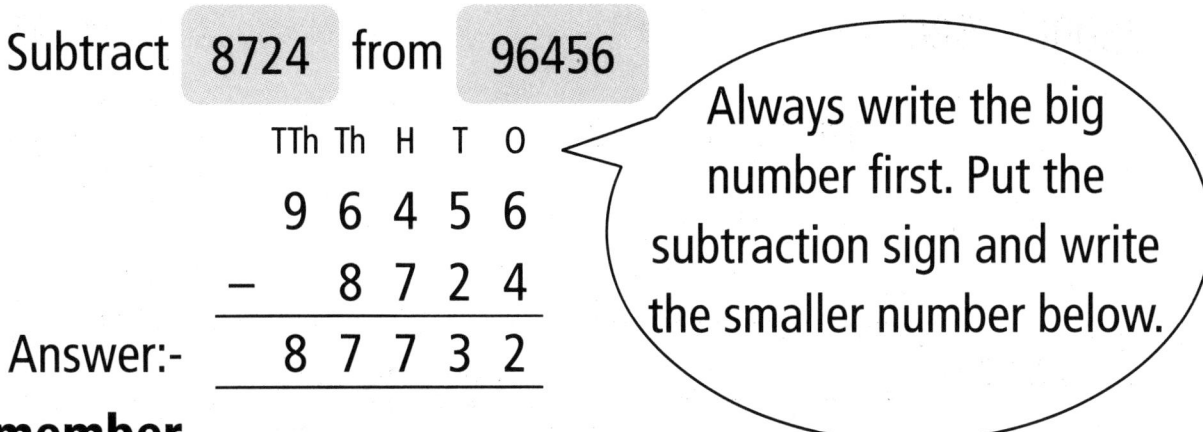

Subtract 8724 from 96456

```
         TTh Th  H  T  O
          9  6  4  5  6
       -        8  7  2  4
         _____
Answer:-  8  7  7  3  2
```

Always write the big number first. Put the subtraction sign and write the smaller number below.

Remember

To check the answers we add the lower number and the number of our answer. If we get the upper number again, it means our answer is absolutely correct!

See the example →

```
    TTh Th  H  T  O
     8  7  7  3  2
  +        8  7  2  4   Lower number
    _____
     9  6  4  5  6   ← Correct answer
```

Now do these subtractions yourself:-

1. 78020 from 88246

```
       TTh Th  H  T  O
        .   .  .  .  .
   +    .   .  .  .  .
       _____
Answer: _____
```

2. 80000 − 58000

        TTh Th H T O

        . . . . .
+ . . . . .
―――――――

Answer: _____

3. 75000 − 580

        TTh Th H T O

        . . . . .
+   . . .
―――――――

Answer: _____

4. 90000 − 9

        TTh Th H T O

        . . . . .
+   .
―――――――

Answer: _____

5. 68000 − 108

        TTh Th H T O

        . . . . .
+   . . .
―――――――

Answer: _____

Multiplication

Multiplication is repeated addition. The sign of multiplication is ×.

$3 \times 6 = \boxed{18}$ means $3 + 3 + 3 + 3 + 3 + 3 = \boxed{18}$

six times three

or

$6 + 6 + 6 = \boxed{18}$

three times six

Remember

Any number multiplied by 1 will be the number itself.

Example:- $6 \times 1 = 6$

$14 \times 1 = 14$

Any number multiplied by 0 will always be **0**.

Example:- $8 \times 0 = 0$

$17 \times 0 = 0$

The number that are being multiplied are called **Factors**. The answer in multiplication is called the **Product**.

Example:-

$$\left.\begin{array}{r} 3\,2 \\ \times\,2 \end{array}\right\} \text{Factors}$$
$$\left.\overline{6\,4}\right\} \text{Product}$$

The product of two numbers does not change, when the order of the number or grouping of the numbers change.

Example:-

$$\left.\begin{array}{r} 10 \times 4 = 40 \\ 4 \times 10 = 40 \end{array}\right] \text{Same number}$$

or

When we multiply, the answer always increases.

Here are two rows of dolls. Each row has five dolls.

So the total number of dolls are 5 + 5 = 10

It means 2 times 5 = 10

In symbols we write 5 + 5 = 2 × 5 = 10

2 × 5 is also read as 5 multiplied by 2

2 times 5 means 2 × 5 = 5 + 5 = 10

Remember that multiplication is the addition of the same number.

Example:-

5 + 5 + 5 = 3 × 5 = 15

5 + 5 + 5 + 5 = 4 × 5 = 20

1 + 1 + 1 + 1 + 1 = 1 × 5 or 5 × 1 = 5

6 + 6 + 6 + 6 + 6 + 6 = 6 × 6 = 36

Multiplication of 2-digit numbers

Example:-

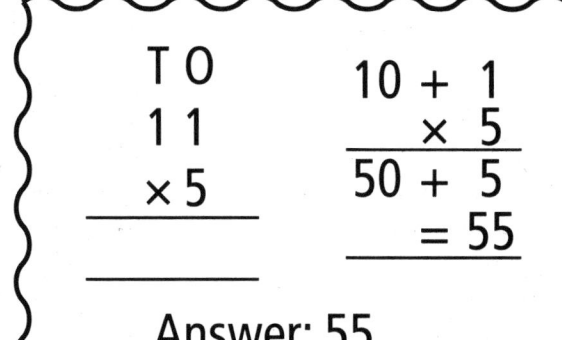

Multiply the ones by 5
Then multiply the tens by 5
Then add both.

Remember
Always use right hand side digit first.

```
  T O        10 + 6
  1 6         × 3
  × 3       -------
 -----       30 + 18
              = 48
Answer: 48
```

Multiply the ones by 3
Then multiply the tens by 3
Then add both.

Multiply:-

1. a. 12   b. 18   c. 42   d. 10
        ×2   ×2   ×2   ×5
        ---   ---   ---   ---
        24

    e. 33   f. 44   g. 11   h. 18
        ×3   ×4   ×6   ×1
        ---   ---   ---   ---

    i. 81   j. 42
        ×8   ×4
        ---   ---

2. Put the following in the repeated addition form.
Example:-

a. 2×2 = 2 + 2 = 4

b. 3×4 = ☐ + ☐ + ☐ = ☐

c. 5×5 = ☐ + ☐ + ☐ + ☐ + ☐ = ☐

d. 5×6 = ☐ + ☐ + ☐ + ☐ + ☐ = ☐

e. 3×7 = ☐ + ☐ + ☐ = ☐

f. 2×8 = ☐ + ☐ = ☐

g. 1×6 = ☐ = ☐

h. 2×4 = ☐ + ☐ = ☐

i. 3×10 = ☐ + ☐ + ☐ = ☐

j. 6×9 = ☐ + ☐ + ☐ + ☐ + ☐ + ☐ = ☐

Remember

$0 \times 2 = 0$

$3 \times 0 = 0$

Any number multiplied by 0 is = 0

$1 \times 5 = 5$

1×5 means 5 taken only once = 5

1×8 means 8 taken only once = 8

So, we observe that 1 multiplied by any number is equal to the number itself.

3. a. 6 × 1 = 6
   b. 12 × 1 = ☐
   c. 1 × 7 = ☐
   d. 16 × 1 = ☐
   e. 12 × 1 = ☐
   f. 1 × 10 = ☐

4. Put these in the multiplication form

   a. 5 + 5 + 5 = 5 × 3 = 15
   b. 1 + 1 + 1 + 1 + 1 + 1 = ☐ × ☐ = ☐
   c. 8 + 8 + 8 + 8 + 8 + 8 = ☐ × ☐ = ☐
   d. 4 + 4 + 4 + 4 = ☐ × ☐ = ☐
   e. 10 + 10 = ☐ × ☐ = ☐

5. Multiplication table of 2
   1. Two one is 2 ⟶ 2 × 1 = 2
   2. Two 2's are 4 ⟶ 2 × 2 = 4
   3. Two 3's are 6 ⟶ 2 × 3 = 6
   4. Two 4's are 8 ⟶ 2 × 4 = 8
   5. Two 5's are 10 ⟶ 2 × 5 = 10
   6. Two 6's are 12 ⟶ 2 × 6 = 12
   7. Two 7's are 14 ⟶ 2 × 7 = 14
   8. Two 8's are 16 ⟶ 2 × 8 = 16
   9. Two 9's are 18 ⟶ 2 × 9 = 18
   10. Two 10's are 20 ⟶ 2 × 10 = 20

   Learn it !

6. **Complete the multiplication table of 5 and 10.**

1 five = 5	1 × 5 = 5	5 × 1 = 5
2 fives = 10	2 × 5 = 10	5 × 2 = 10
3 fives = 15	3 × 5 = 15	5 × 3 = 15
4 fives = 20	4 × 5 = ☐	☐ × 4 = ☐
5 fives = 25	☐ × 5 = ☐	☐ × 5 = ☐
6 fives = 30	☐ × 5 = ☐	☐ × 6 = ☐
7 fives = 35	☐ × 5 = ☐	☐ × 7 = ☐
8 fives = 40	☐ × 5 = ☐	☐ × 8 = ☐
9 fives = 45	☐ × 5 = ☐	☐ × 9 = ☐
10 fives = 50	☐ × 5 = ☐	☐ × 10 = ☐

7. **Table of 10**

1 Tens = 10	1 × 10 = 10	10 × 1 = 10
2 Tens = 20	2 × 10 = 20	10 × 2 = 20
3 Tens = 30	3 × 10 = 30	10 × 3 = 30
4 Tens = 40	☐ × 10 = ☐	10 × ☐ = ☐
5 Tens = 40	☐ × 10 = ☐	10 × ☐ = ☐
6 Tens = 40	☐ × 10 = ☐	10 × ☐ = ☐
7 Tens = 40	☐ × 10 = ☐	10 × ☐ = ☐
8 Tens = 40	☐ × 10 = ☐	10 × ☐ = ☐
9 Tens = 40	☐ × 10 = ☐	10 × ☐ = ☐
10 Tens = 40	☐ × 10 = ☐	10 × ☐ = ☐

Think and Tell

Fill up the blanks.

1. The smallest one-digit number is — `1`
2. The largest one-digit number is — `9`
3. The smallest two-digit number is — ☐
4. The largest two-digit number is — ☐
5. The smallest three-digit number is — ☐
6. The largest three-digit number is — ☐
7. The smallest four-digit number is — ☐
8. What comes after 799? — ☐
9. What comes before 600? — ☐
10. What comes between 49 and 51? — ☐
11. What will be the number if we less one number from ninety? — ☐
12. What will be the number if we add 2 numbers to ninety nine? — ☐
13. What will be the answer if 2 is multiplied 4 times — ☐
14. Write the total number when 400 is added to 99 and one? (400 + 99 + 1) — ☐
15. Which number is the greatest 12, 345, 54, 321? — ☐

Ordinal Numbers

Ordinal numbers are those which denote sequence or position like first and second.

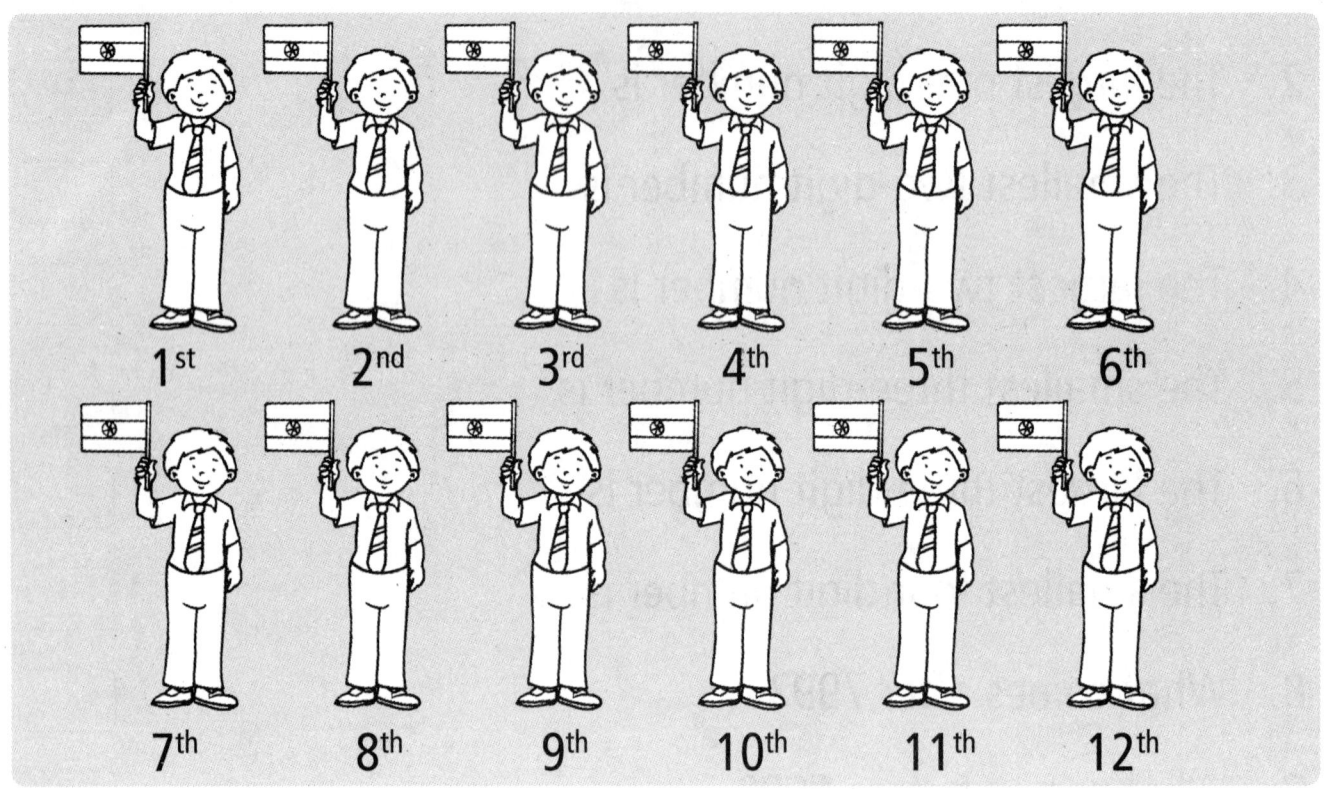

Cardinal Numbers

Cardinal numbers are those which denote quantity such as 1 and 2.

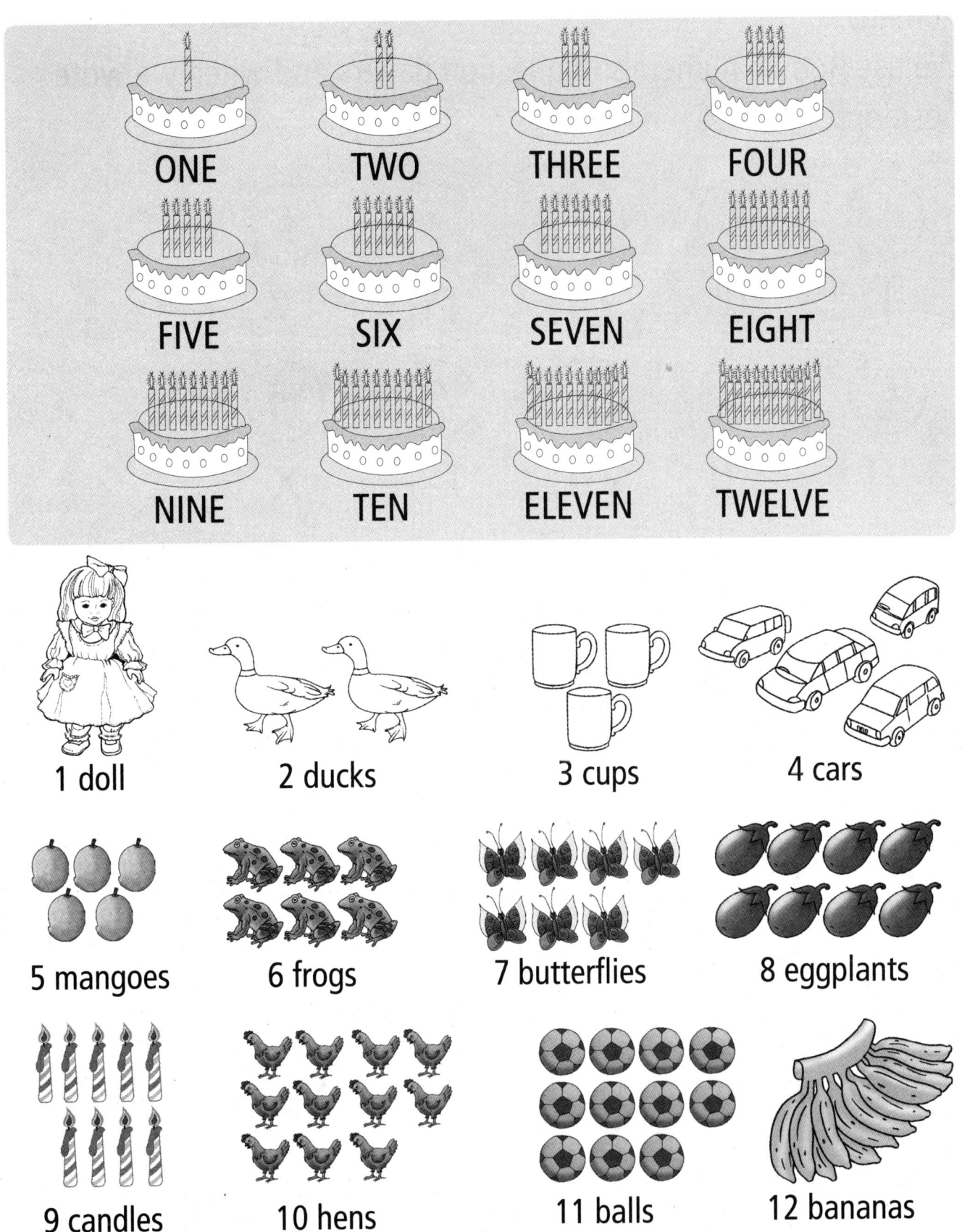

Roman Numerals

It is a system of numbering which we have got from the ancient Romans.

We use Roman numerals in question papers and when we write positions.

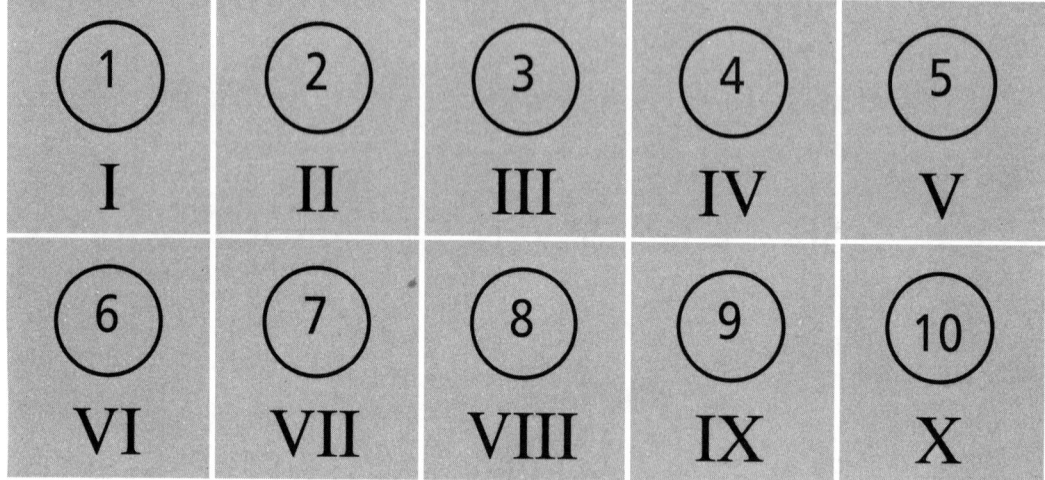

Roman numbers	I	V	X	L	C	D	M
Indo-arabic numerals	1	5	10	50	100	500	1000

1. Make a circle on the alphabets which are used in Roman numerals.

A	B	C	D	E	F	G	H
ⓘ	J	K	L	M	N	O	P
Q	R	S	T	U	V	W	X
Y	Z						

2. Use match sticks and write the following Roman numerals.

a.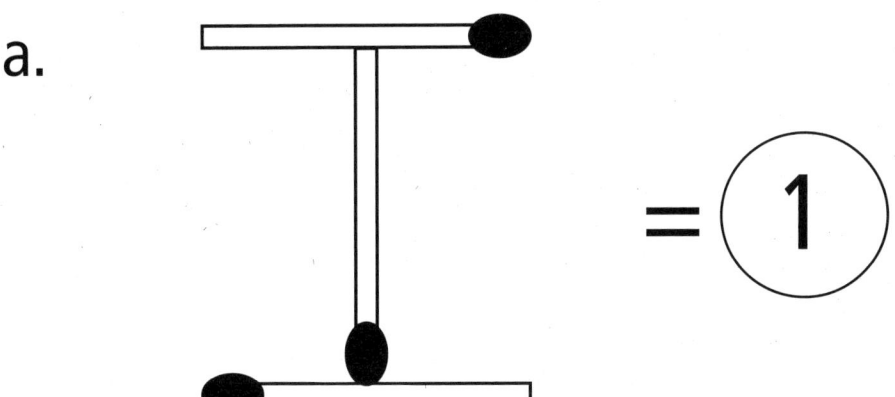

b.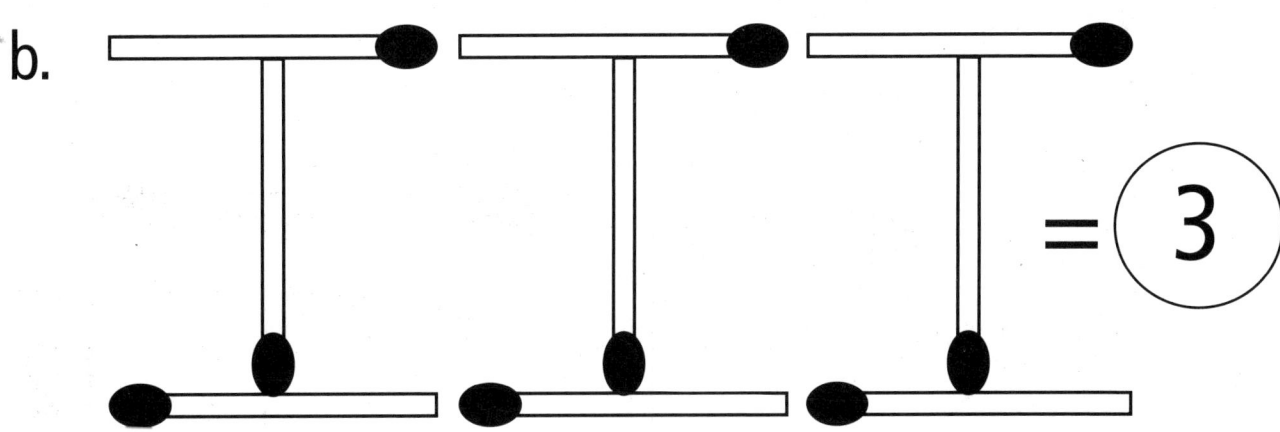

c.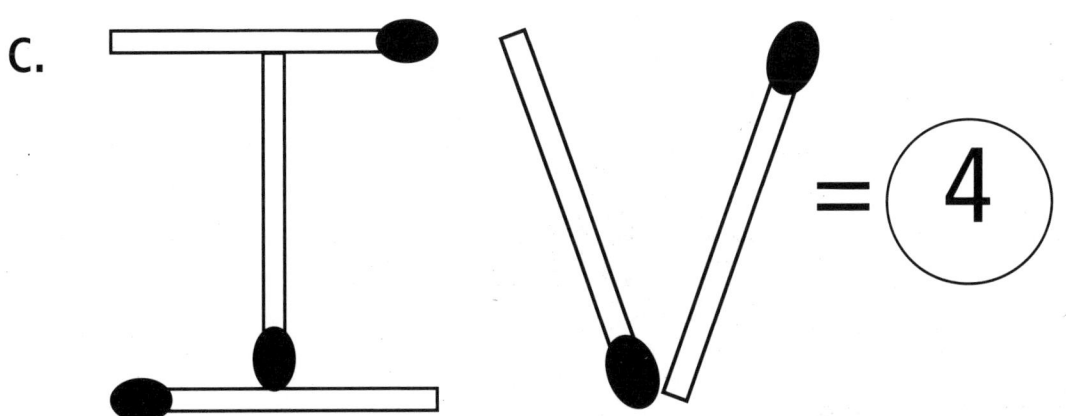

d. 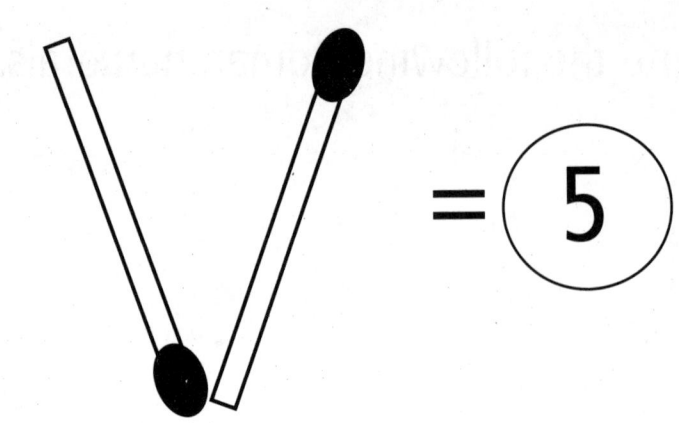 = 5

e. 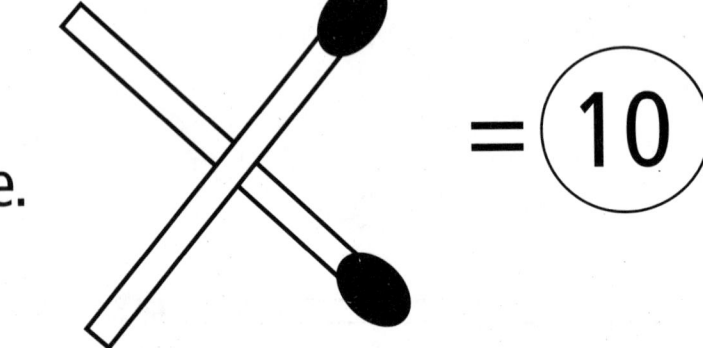 = 10

f. 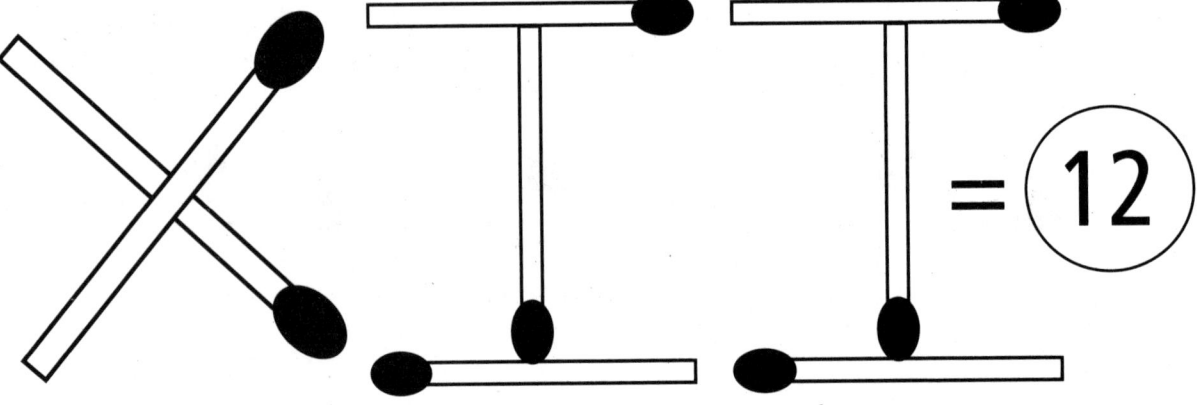 = 12

g. 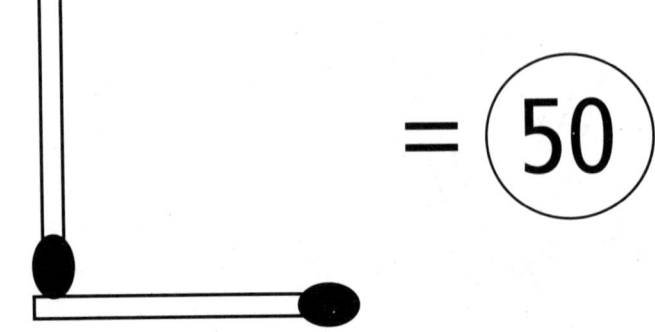 = 50

Time

We use clocks to see the time. The long hand as you know denotes minutes and the short hand denotes hours.

1. Draw hands to show the given time in the clocks.

Twenty five past six   8 O' clock   Half past ten   Quarter to three

2. Write the time in words and figures.

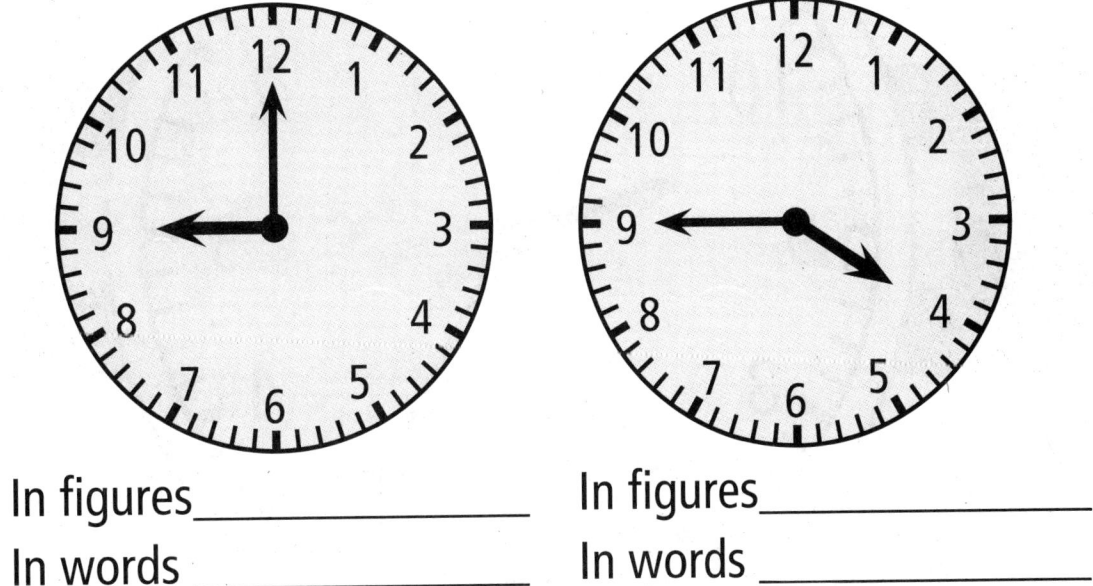

In figures_____   In figures_____
In words _____   In words _____

3. Fill up the blanks.
    a. There are _____ minutes in 1 hour.
    b. There are _____ seconds in one minute.
    c. 60 _____ make one hour.
    d. In the morning my school starts at 8.00 _____ (pm/am).

Calculating Time

Learn to calculate the time.

1. Aman is waiting for a train. How many minutes the long hand of his watch will cover if it reaches from number 12 to number 5? His train's arrival time was 9.00 am. But the train reached late when the small hand of the watch was on 9 and the long hand was on 5. How many minutes the train was late?

   Answer: The train was ☐ minutes late.

2. How much time do you take to reach school from your house, can you tell?

Answer: I take _____ minutes to reach my school from my house

Writing in Figures

Write these numbers in figures.

1. Fourteen = ☐

2. Four hundred and seven = ☐

3. Twelve hundred = ☐

4. One thousand two hundred = ☐

5. Six hundred and forty = ☐

6. Six thousand and eighty = ☐

7. Nine thousand ten = ☐

8. Eight thousand eighty = ☐

9. Four thousand three hundred and two = ☐

10. Six hundred and seven = ☐

11. Seven hundred five hundred and one = ☐

Type of Straight Lines

Straight lines can be drawn in different ways.
Example:-

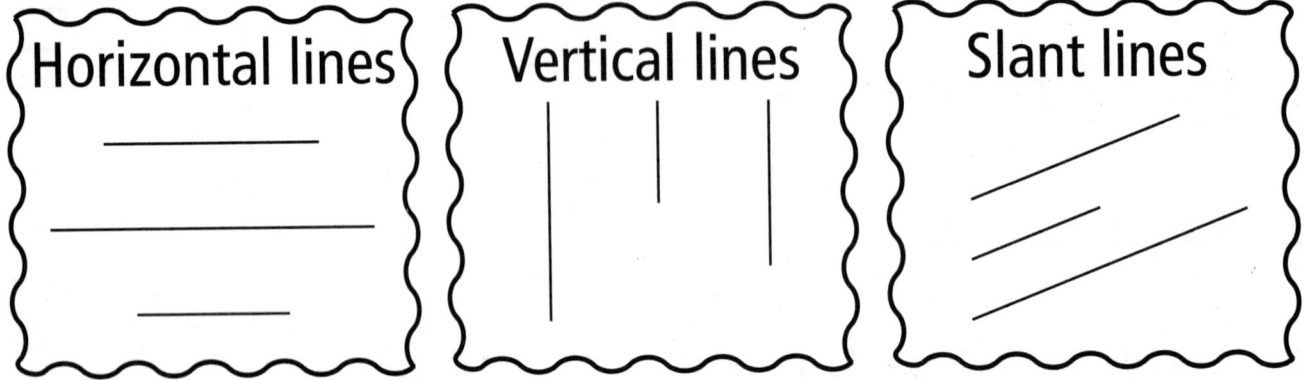

Here are a few dotted figures. Join the dots and see what shapes you get.

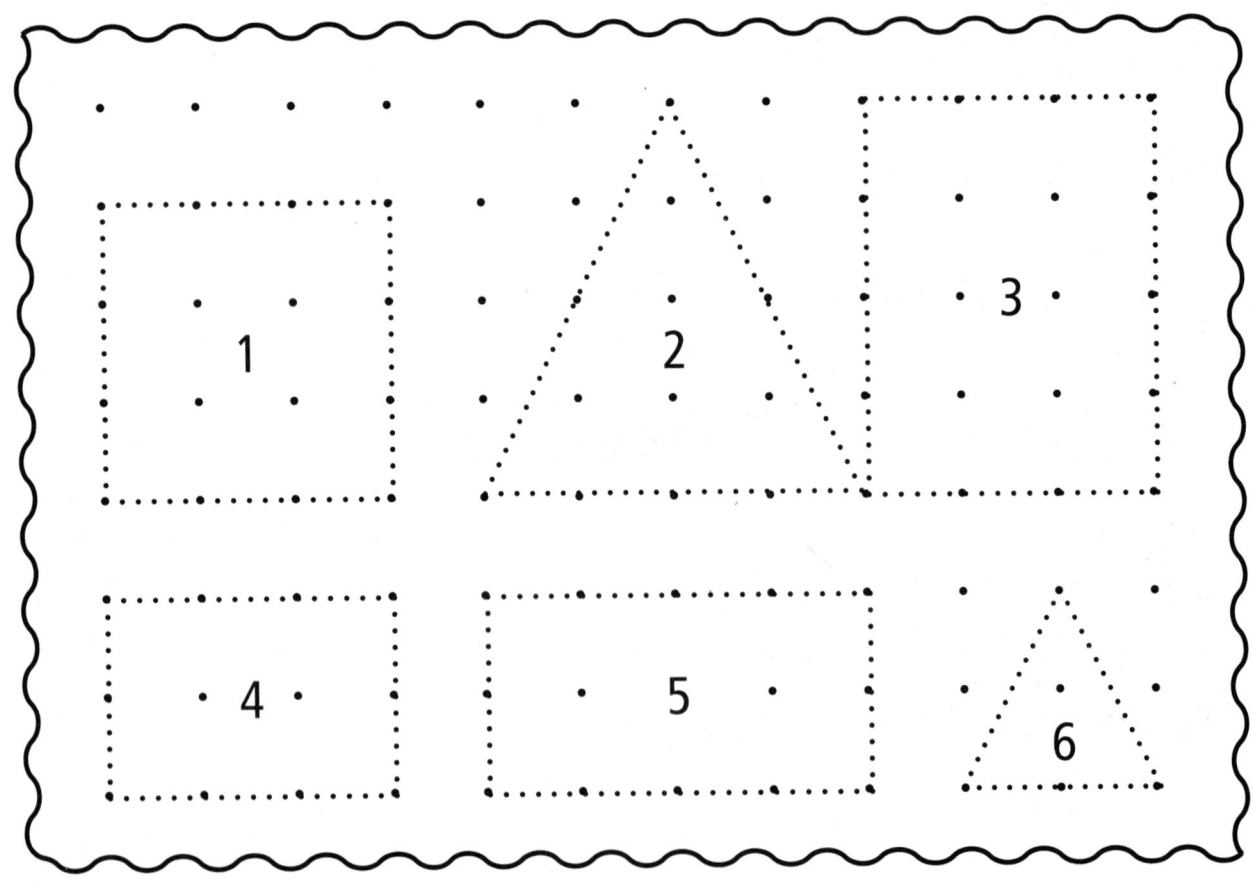

Building of Numbers

Remember
- To build the greatest number, rearrange the digits in the decreasing order.
- To build the smallest number, rearrange the digits in the increasing order.
- We do not write 0 at the beginning of a number.

Example:-

(a) Greatest number = 97640   (Decreasing order)
(b) Smallest number = 40679   (Increasing order)

1. Built the smallest and the greatest 5-digit number with the number given below write the number name of each.

Remember
We do not begin a number with 0.

a. 8   0   7   9   3

Smallest number = ☐

= _____

Greatest number = ☐

= _____

b.

Smallest number = ☐

= _____

Greatest number = ☐

= _____

c.

Smallest number = ☐

= _____

Greatest number = ☐

= _____

d.

Smallest number = ☐

= _____

Greatest number = ☐

= _____

e.

Smallest number = ☐

= _____

Greatest number = ☐

= _____

f.

Smallest number = ☐

= _____

Greatest number = ☐

= _____

Division

Division is the process of dividing something. The sign of division (÷) shows that the number which comes before it is to be divided by the number which comes after it. So division is the opposite of multiplication.

Example:- Here are 2 groups of boys. Each group has six members:

First group   Second group

How many boys are altogether there?
Answer: 6 + 6 = (12) Total people.
or
6 × 2 = (12) peoples
Now divide 12 people into 3 equal group:
Answer: 12 ÷ 3 = 4
Answer: (4) people in each group.

If 16 apples are shared equally among 4 children, how many apples each child will get?

Example:-

From the above figure it is clear that each child will get 4 apples. It shows that division means to share in parts.

We can write like this—

$16 \div 4 = 4$

We know that $4 \times 4 = 16$

So division is the opposite of multiplication.

We can write : $16 \div 4 = 4$

or

$$4\overline{)16}\,\,4$$
$$\underline{-16}$$
$$\times$$

Answer: Each child will get 4 apples.

Divisions have 4 parts. Learn their names.
Divide 45 by 5:-

$$\text{Divisor} \leftarrow 5 \overline{\smash{)}\begin{array}{r} 9 \text{ (Quotient)} \\ 45 \text{ (Dividend)} \\ -45 \\ \hline 0 \text{ (Remainder)} \end{array}}$$

$$\text{Divisor} \leftarrow 8 \overline{\smash{)}\begin{array}{r} 10 \text{ (Quotient)} \\ 80 \text{ (Dividend)} \\ -80 \\ \hline 0 \text{ (Remainder)} \end{array}}$$

$$\text{Divisor} \leftarrow 8 \overline{\smash{)}\begin{array}{r} 8 \text{ (Quotient)} \\ 66 \text{ (Dividend)} \\ -64 \\ \hline 2 \text{ (Remainder)} \end{array}}$$

- **Remember**: Divident ÷ Divisor = Divisor = Quotient
  a. 45 ÷ 5 = 9
  b. 80 ÷ 8 = 10

- Divisor × Quotient = Dividend
  a. 5 × 9 = 45
  b. 8 × 10 = 80

1. Do the given divisions in your notebook.

   1. $8\overline{)81}$
   2. $11\overline{)110}$
   3. $8\overline{)64}$
   4. $9\overline{)49}$
   5. $7\overline{)56}$
   6. $10\overline{)120}$
   7. $10\overline{)100}$
   8. $8\overline{)72}$

2. Divide the given objects into parts in the space provided. One has been done for you.

   Divide 16 flowers in two pots

   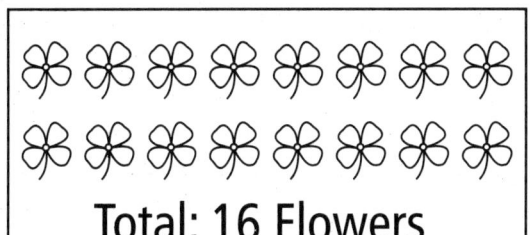 $16 \div 2 =$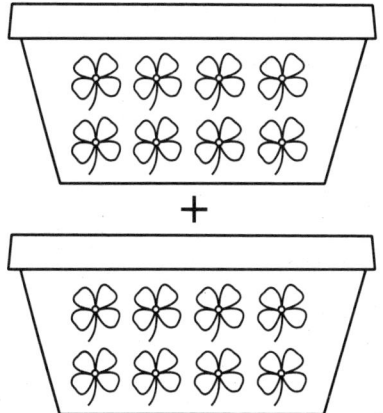

   Answer: 8 flowers in each pot.

   a. Divide 2 dozen pencils among 4 children. How many pencils each will get?

   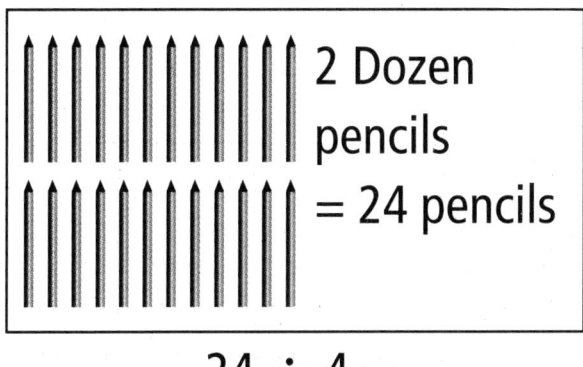

   $24 \div 4 =$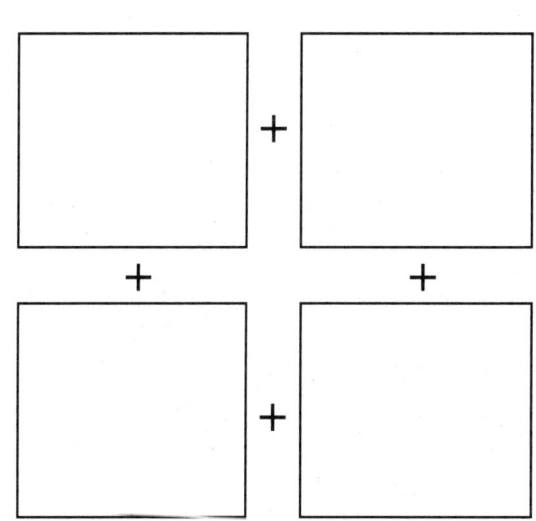

   Answer: Each child will get ☐ pencils.

   b. Distribute one packet of toffees among five boys. The packet has 100 toffees in it.

   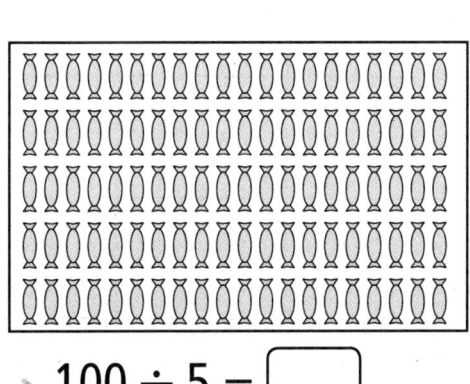

   $100 \div 5 =$ ☐

   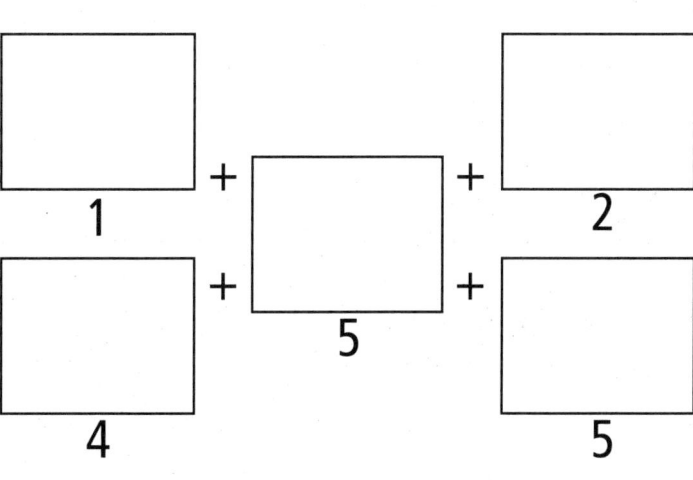

3. Divide and write the dividend, divisor, quotient and remainder. One has been done for you

S. N.	Divide	Dividend	Divisor	Quotient	Remainder
a.	$50 \div 7 = 7$, R = 1	50	7	7	1
b.	$64 \div 10 = 6$, R = 4				
c.	$45 \div 7 = \square$, R = $\square$				
d.	$83 \div 7 = \square$, R = $\square$				
e.	$108 \div 7 = \square$, R = $\square$				
f.	$74 \div 8 = \square$, R = $\square$				
g.	$59 \div 7 = \square$, R = $\square$				
h.	$42 \div 6 = \square$, R = $\square$				
i.	$99 \div 10 = \square$, R = $\square$				
j.	$100 \div 11 = \square$, R = $\square$				
k.	$41 \div 4 = \square$, R = $\square$				
l.	$79 \div 8 = \square$, R = $\square$				

Recognising Numbers

1. Colour the bigger number

39

40

2. Circle the smallest number.
   a. 60, 37, 47, 16, 14, 40
   b. 27, 36, 49, 19, 20, 12
   c. 15, 16, 67, 57, 29, 20

3. Tick the greatest number.
   a. 80, 18, 20, 46, 97
   b. 84, 78, 89, 69, 39

4. Circle the odd numbers.
   a. 20, 13, 14, 6, 12
   b. 14, 15, 18, 8, 10
   c. 20, 17, 80, 94, 100
   d. 98, 40, 23, 66, 50

Tease your Brain

1. You have bought a chocolate costing Rs. 28 and 100gm of butter costing Rs. 22. Give a 100 rupee note to the shopkeeper. How much money will he return?

Answer: The shopkeeper will return Rs. ☐

2. Take 10 coins of Rs. 5 and add the amount.
   a. How much money do you have now?

Answer: Total money = Rs. ☐

   b. If you wish to purchase a box of cookies worth Rs. 25, how many coins you will give to the shopkeeper?

Answer: ☐ coins

   c. How many coins left with you?

Answer: ☐ coins

   d. How much money you have now?

Answer: Rs. ☐

Making a Calendar

Write the dates of the current month.

Sunday	
Monday	
Tuesday	
Wednesday	
Thursday	
Friday	
Saturday	

Now tell:-

1. From which day is the current month beginning?

Answer: ☐

2. How many Sundays are there in this month?

Answer: ☐

3. How many weeks are there in this month?

Answer: ☐

Making Patterns

Material required:-

Matchsticks   Fevicol

Procedure:-

Make the given patterns using matchsticks.

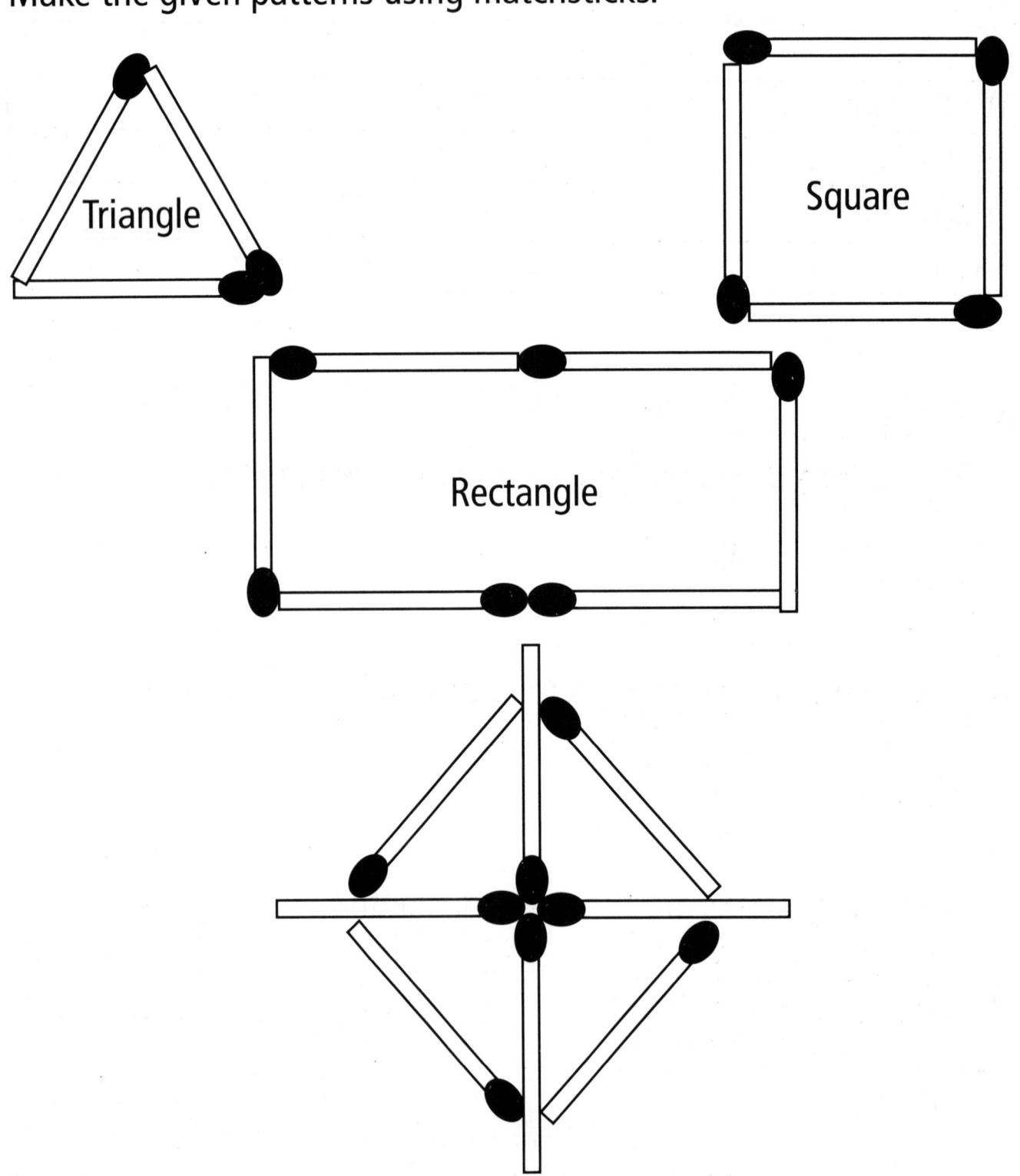

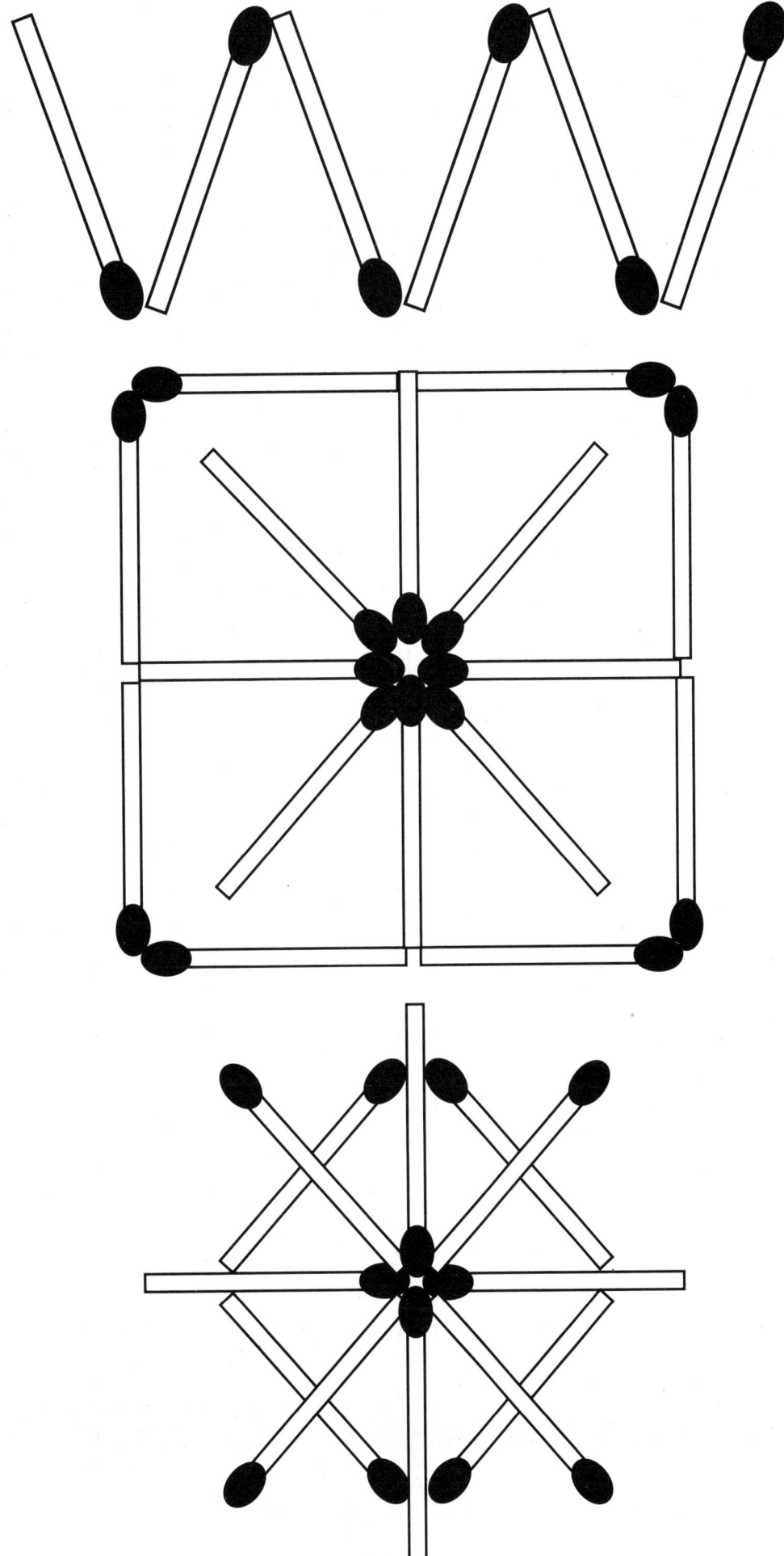

Bar Graph

Here is a table which shows the records of story books children borrowed from the central Library in 2010.

Month	Numbers of books borrowed	Month	Numbers of books borrowed
January	28	July	10
February	16	August	30
March	18	September	32
April	20	October	14
May	30	November	12
June	28	December	16

Complete the vertical bar graph in the space below to represent the information shown in the table.

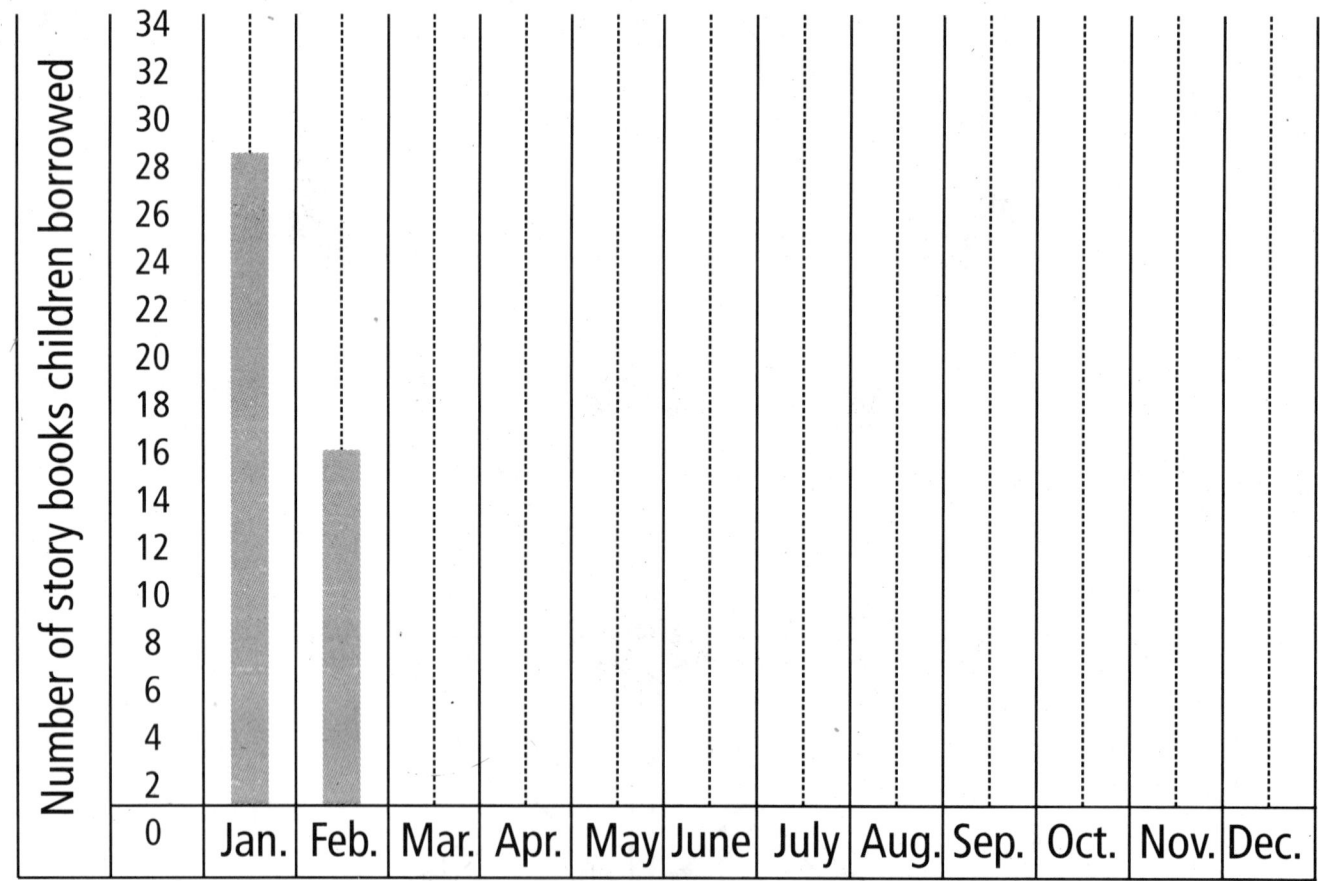

Month
Year 2010